*A tale of two*
# CATHEDRALS
**OLD SARUM · NEW SALISBURY**

*Peter Brimacombe*

ENGLISH HERITAGE

1997

# CONTENTS

Text Copyright © 1997 Peter Brimacombe

First published 1997 by English Heritage, 23 Savile Row, London W1X 1AB

Designed by The Sainsbury Lavero Design Partnership.
Printed by White Dove Press.
ISBN 1 85074 677 X
Product code XD20012

*A catalogue record of this publication is available from the British Library.*

# INTRODUCTION

A TALE of two cathedrals spans more than 900 years, from the building of the first Romanesque cathedral on the windswept heights of Salisbury Plain, not long after the Norman Conquest, to the great Early English ecclesiastical masterpiece that graces the city of Salisbury today.

A tale of two cathedrals explains how a cathedral came to be founded within an ancient Iron Age hillfort, what prompted the move to the new site, and how this was ultimately achieved.

'Let us descend joyfully to the plains where the valleys abound with corn, where the fields are beautiful and where there is freedom from oppression,' cried Peter de Blois, one of the more eloquent canons.

History is invariably a consequence of human endeavour. The story of the two cathedrals was shaped by the great kings and clergy of medieval England, while the architecture represents genius and creative craftsmanship of the highest order.

# IN THE BEGINNING

OLD SARUM: *Roman whistle pipe carved from a small bone. (English Heritage/Salisbury Museum)*

**S**ALISBURY PLAIN is an ancient landscape, settled by man beyond the horizon of recorded time and subsequently trampled over by almost every army that has succeeded in invading our shores. Some of the earliest buildings created many thousands of years ago – Avebury, Stonehenge, Silbury Hill – still loom large across the Wiltshire countryside, while burial grounds such as the West Kennet long barrow are considered even older. The Wandsdyke straggles over hill and dale marking territorial frontiers, and the Ridgeway was one of England's first ever long-distance cross-country routes.

The early primitive hunters gave way to Neolithic farmers, who grew Wiltshire's first grain crops between 4000 and 2500 BC. When the invaders arrived from the continent during the Iron Age, protection was needed from hostile incursions, so hillforts such as those at Figsbury Ring and Yarnbury Castle were developed in the neighbourhood, as well as Old Sarum itself. These hillforts provided a safe haven against attack, and also acted as administrative centres, cattle pounds, and places for regular markets. Most were abandoned after the Romans left, but Old Sarum is unique in this part of Wessex in that it was later occupied by the Saxons.

The Romans introduced a more sophisticated way of life to the area, but the legions' departure shortly after AD 400 created total chaos as 'Pax Romana' swiftly evaporated and the native Britons, Anglo-Saxon newcomers, and marauding Danes fought over the territory with relentless ferocity. Civilisation was in darkness, yet a faint flickering candle of Christianity survived in the far west of Britain,

STONEHENGE: *General view inside stone circle.*
*(English Heritage)*

kept alive by two great Celtic saints, St Patrick and St Columba. According to the early twelfth-century historian William of Malmesbury, the former visited Glastonbury, while the latter's exploits caused Pope Gregory to dispatch St Augustine to Britain 1400 years ago to convert the pagan Kentish king. 'Inspired by God to send his servant Augustine with several other God-fearing monks to preach the word of God to the English nation,' wrote the Venerable Bede, describing the hazardous journey which led to the foundation of the first archbishop's cathedral at Canterbury.

J. M. W. TURNER: *Salisbury from Old Sarum.*
*(Salisbury Museum)*

There was a brief period of respite in the ninth century when one of the nation's more robust legendary heroes, Alfred the Great, became King of Wessex. Alfred battled with the invading Danes at Wilton, then more important than Old Sarum, and later decisively defeated these persistent invaders at Edington, near Westbury.

Alfred strengthened the defences at Old Sarum and is thought to have established the nunnery at Wilton Abbey on the site of the present day Wilton House. Two of his elder brothers were buried at Sherborne Abbey, the late Anglo-Saxon monastic cathedral founded in AD 705 by St Aldhelm, its first bishop.

While momentous events were happening all around, little of real note occurred at Old Sarum, constantly changing ownership merely reflected in a change of name, the Celtic *Sorviadun*, 'the fortress by the gentle river', giving way to the Roman *Sorbiodunum*, then becoming *Searobyrh* in the Anglo-Saxon Chronicles.

All was about to change, as in several successive centuries a series of exceptional men were to thrust firstly Old Sarum and then Salisbury firmly to the centre stage of English history.

DEVIL'S DEN:
*Clatford.*
*(Peter Brimacombe)*

# INTO THE MIDDLE AGES

URING the first half of the eleventh century England had been enjoying a relatively peaceful period and the fortunes of the little Saxon town of Old Sarum had prospered accordingly. Yet the loosely knit kingdom of the unworldly Edward the Confessor was in decline, and across the Channel a new military power was growing into a mighty force destined to have a profound impact on both Old Sarum and England as a whole.

GOLD RING *found near Old Sarum, bearing the name of King Ethelwulf of Wessex. (British Museum)*

Four years after William the Conqueror's army had annihilated the Saxons in 1066 at the Battle of Hastings, William had gained ascendancy throughout the entire country and decided to disband his army at Old Sarum, paying them off with captured Saxon treasure. William had chosen Old Sarum for this symbolic event on account of its central location in the south of England, at a point where several major roads converged. The Normans had been quick to appreciate the tactical defensive capability of the ancient hillfort together with its strategic potential for controlling the surrounding area. They had already begun to build their first castle, a small group of buildings initially constructed of wood, sited on

TWELFTH-CENTURY STONE CARVINGS *from Bishop Roger's cathedral. (English Heritage/Salisbury Museum)*

the steep mound and surrounded by a wooden stockade. These were progressively replaced in stone during the twelfth century, while the surrounding town grew and prospered amid the enforced stability of Norman rule.

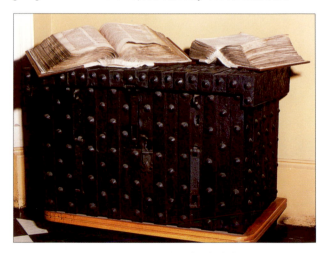

DOMESDAY BOOK *resting on the chest in which it was kept from the seventeenth century. (Public Record Office)*

TWELFTH-CENTURY STONE CARVING *from Bishop Roger's Cathedral. (English Heritage/Salisbury Museum)*

In 1085 a renewed threat of invasion from the Danes caused William to initiate a thorough assessment of the wealth and resources of his kingdom. This wide-ranging census of the nation came to be known as the Domesday Book, part of which was compiled by the clerks of the embryonic cathedral at Old Sarum, which was being constructed at that time, and closely supervised by Bishop Osmund, previously Chancellor to the king. Speed was of the essence and this incredibly detailed survey was completed within one year. On the first day of August 1086, William summoned to Old Sarum 'all the landholding men of any account throughout England, whosoever they were', in order to swear an oath of allegiance to their king. It is said that a crowd numbering 60,000 appeared before William the Conqueror at Old Sarum on that day.

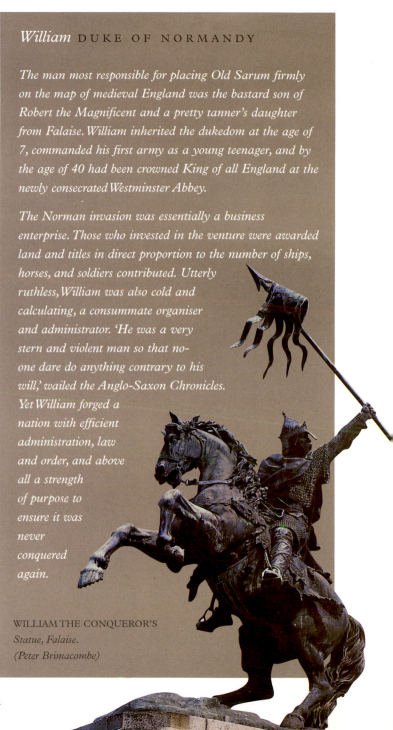

### *William* DUKE OF NORMANDY

*The man most responsible for placing Old Sarum firmly on the map of medieval England was the bastard son of Robert the Magnificent and a pretty tanner's daughter from Falaise. William inherited the dukedom at the age of 7, commanded his first army as a young teenager, and by the age of 40 had been crowned King of all England at the newly consecrated Westminster Abbey.*

*The Norman invasion was essentially a business enterprise. Those who invested in the venture were awarded land and titles in direct proportion to the number of ships, horses, and soldiers contributed. Utterly ruthless, William was also cold and calculating, a consummate organiser and administrator. 'He was a very stern and violent man so that no-one dare do anything contrary to his will,' wailed the Anglo-Saxon Chronicles. Yet William forged a nation with efficient administration, law and order, and above all a strength of purpose to ensure it was never conquered again.*

WILLIAM THE CONQUEROR'S *Statue, Falaise. (Peter Brimacombe)*

DETAIL FROM
*Sarum Psalter.*
*(Salisbury Cathedral Library)*

# THE FIRST CATHEDRAL

A DECADE after the Battle of Hastings, the whole of England was under William's control and an intense period of indoctrination into the Norman way of life was under way right across the nation. William was a deeply religious man, so reforming the English Church was high on his agenda. His long-standing friend Lanfranc had replaced the Anglo-Saxon Stigand as Archbishop of Canterbury and in 1075 he summoned the bishops to St Paul's Cathedral. At this Council of London it was finally decided to relocate cathedrals from the mainly rural locations which they had hitherto occupied to more urban sites. This far-reaching decision resulted in the see (or diocese) of Sherborne, which had previously been combined with that of Ramsbury in Berkshire, becoming that of Old Sarum.

William of Malmesbury had been particularly scathing about the cathedral located at Sherborne: 'a small village agreeable neither for the density of its population nor for the attraction of its position, in which it is a cause for wonder and almost shame that an episcopal see lasted so many centuries.' William was equally puzzled about the choice of Old Sarum – 'a castle instead of a town'. He was unaware that political considerations, location, and security were the deciding factors.

Herman, hitherto Bishop of Sherborne, of Flemish origins and once chaplain to Edward the Confessor, obediently moved to the new site inside the old Iron Age hillfort, but died before much progress could be made. His successor, Osmund, began the construction of one of the earliest cathedrals in England created in the Romanesque style, part of a huge surge of ecclesiastical building when dozens of new cathedrals and abbey churches were created across the nation.

Building of the cathedral began around 1075, and it was consecrated in 1092 on a site in the north-west corner of the old Saxon town close to the new Norman keep, a factor that was to cause considerable difficulty in the future. The building followed the typical Norman style of having three apse-ended spaces separated by the solid walls of the choir. While its overall appearance was no doubt revolutionary in the neighbourhood, it was not as distinguished or as large as other cathedrals under construction elsewhere in England at that time.

While Sherborne had been served by Benedictine monks, the new cathedral at Old Sarum was destined to be a 'secular foundation' run by canons under the auspices of four principals – dean, precentor, chancellor, and treasurer. These four offices – older than that of the Chancellor of the Exchequer – remain today. The organisational procedures instigated by Bishop Osmund formed part of what later became known as the 'Use of Sarum', a concept for the organisation of religious services and the administration of cathedral life, later adopted by other great secular foundations such as Exeter, Chichester,

Lincoln, and York. Only five days after the cathedral had been consecrated it was struck by lightning and badly damaged, much to the horror of the highly superstitious clergy who saw this calamity as an inauspicious omen.

CAPITAL 'A' *from a tenth-century manuscript in the library.*
*(Salisbury Cathedral Library)*

## Medieval MANUSCRIPTS

*William of Malmesbury records Osmund's passion for scholarship. He greatly encouraged the creation of manuscripts, even helping to write and bind them himself. They were subsequently brought to the new cathedral in Salisbury and are now maintained in the Cathedral Library, forming the largest collection of late eleventh- and early twelfth-century manuscripts surviving from one source in England. There are some 200 manuscripts in total in the library which date from the ninth to the fifteenth century, more than 50 of which were produced at Old Sarum. The tenth-century illuminated Salisbury Psalter is particularly remarkable.*

MANUSCRIPT *written up at Old Sarum in the late eleventh century.*
*(Salisbury Cathedral Library)*

# PORTRAIT OF A SAINT

**T**HEY weep today in Salisbury, for he is dead. Who was the sword of justice and father of Salisbury's church.

In his strength he cherished the wretched; he feared not the pride of the great.

But was a strong mace, the terror of evil-doers. He took his descent from dukes and men of noble birth.

And in his time, jewel-like, reflected on the princes of his house.

This epitaph records the death in the last year of the eleventh century of Salisbury Cathedral's most venerated bishop, the man who built the first cathedral at Old Sarum and whose remains were brought to the new Salisbury Cathedral in 1226. He was canonised by the Pope on January 1, 1457.

Osmund's reputation shines down the centuries with the saintly glow of a medieval stained-glass window. As is so often the case, his origins are obscure. He is thought to have been born in Normandy in the mid eleventh century, perhaps of noble birth and possibly the nephew of William the Conqueror. He may have been educated at the renowned monastery of Bec, which under Lanfranc had become the foremost centre of learning in Western Europe. Certainly Osmund came to England in the wake of the Norman Conquest to take up office in the Royal Court, later becoming William's Chancellor. When Bishop

Herman died in 1078, Lanfranc, by then Archbishop of Canterbury, consecrated Osmund as Bishop at Sarum.

The Council of London had decreed that the old cathedral of Sherborne must be resited at Old Sarum. By this time the Norman grip on Saxon England was becoming progressively tighter – even repressive and humiliating. Osmund, however, adopted a more enlightened and compassionate approach and his ready acknowledgement of the miracle associated with the Saxon St Aldhelm won him the gratitude of his oppressed diocese, where he could also be found addressing rustic congregations in faltering English.

PART OF A SHRINE, *thought to be St Osmund's.*
*(Salisbury Cathedral Works Department)*

Osmund was renowned for his intellectual powers. He was determined to make Old Sarum a scholastic centre of excellence in a country hitherto regarded as a complete cultural backwater. He recruited clerks, 'distinguished for their learning', to assemble the large collection of manuscripts that still survives today. William of Malmesbury admired the canons at Old Sarum who 'outshone all others for their chant', while John of Salisbury, who originally gained his learning at Old Sarum, was to become one of the most distinguished scholars of his day, and eventually Bishop of Chartres.

Osmund was an austere man in the same mould as Bernard of Clairvaux. He was a strict, unrelenting disciplinarian who took piety to the point of obsession, particularly in his desire to enforce celibacy and chastity among his clergy. William of Malmesbury comments that Osmund, 'seemed harsher than was just to penitents, when he punished more severely in others sins which he did not find in himself.' Certainly, Osmund's dismissal of a highly educated canon named Goscelin, who had formed an affectionate yet innocent relationship with a nun at nearby Wilton Abbey, seems an act of near fanatical zeal that was to sour relationships permanently between the bishop and the abbess, despite the intervention of Archbishop Anselm.

Eventually the virtuous Osmund was to contract 'an earthly disease and was wasted away before his death by a long illness'. For 21 years he had been Bishop at Old Sarum and of the cathedral which he had created.

Nearly 900 years later Osmund's tomb lies in the present cathedral, his memory providing inspiration to every bishop who has succeeded him.

DRAWING OF OSMUND *binding books.*
*(Salisbury Cathedral Works Department)*

# THE HEYDAY OF OLD SARUM

OSMUND'S successor at Old Sarum was the rather less saintly Bishop Roger. Whereas the pious Osmund had rigidly enforced celibacy among his clergy, Roger openly maintained a mistress, Matilda of Ramsbury. The highly talented and ambitious Roger rose from lowly beginnings in Avranches to become one of those Norman high priests who could move effortlessly from cloister to the corridors of power. In addition to his ecclesiastical post, Roger was Henry I's Chancellor and later Justiciar, one of the most powerful men in the kingdom, rumoured to have first gained royal favour by possessing the happy ability to conduct mass in a shorter time than any other priest before the king went hunting!

BISHOP ROGER'S *tomb.*
*(Salisbury Cathedral Works Department)*

Roger energetically set about rebuilding and enlarging his cathedral, extending eastwards, giving it a square-ended choir with aisles, an ambulatory, and three chapels including a long square-ended Lady Chapel. He added a new west end too, and a crypt and cloister together with a magnificent Bishop's Palace.

In addition, the cathedral was adorned with some of the finest Romanesque sculpture in England, and possessed a highly colourful interior with an elaborate floor so exceptional that only two others like it survive in the country, at Canterbury and Westminster. Fragments of Old Sarum's floor can now be seen in the Salisbury Museum. 'He built anew the church at Salisbury and beautified it in such a manner that it yielded to none in England but surpasses many', declared William of Malmesbury approvingly. Meanwhile, a grateful king gave Roger the command of the castle and the town prospered amid the bishop's continuing power and popularity.

All went well until Henry died in the winter of 1135 and his nephew Stephen promptly usurped the throne which had been promised to Henry's daughter Maud, thereby plunging the country into a prolonged and bitter civil war. Stephen imprisoned Roger in 1139, suspecting him of siding with Maud, and at the same time

BISHOP JOCELYN *and seal.*
*(Salisbury Museum)*
*Both Bishop Roger's and Bishop Jocelyn's tombs were moved from the old cathedral to the new one in 1226.*

repossessed the castle. Roger died in disgrace shortly afterwards and neither his successor, Jocelyn, bishop for more than 40 years, nor any subsequent bishop of Old Sarum ever controlled the castle again. This was a growing source of friction between the royal garrison and the clergy of the adjacent cathedral, a microcosm of the growing acrimony developing between Church and Crown, in particular the bitter feud between Henry II and the forceful Archbishop of Canterbury, Thomas à Becket.

Jocelyn had also quarrelled with Becket and was twice excommunicated. He was even suspected of being implicated in the brutal murder of Becket at Canterbury in the winter of 1170, but was subsequently able to clear himself and obtain papal absolution. The first church built in the new town of Salisbury was later to be dedicated to Thomas à Becket. After Jocelyn had retired to a Cistercian monastery, Herbert Poore was elected bishop, but because he was illegitimate – ' quia de concubina natus est' – his appointment was not confirmed. Hubert Walter became bishop instead. It was only after Walter had been appointed Archbishop of Canterbury that Herbert Poore was successful in becoming Bishop of Old Sarum in 1194, an appointment gladly ratified by his predecessor. Walter was another man in Holy Orders skilled in other forms of high office. He was Justiciar to Richard I, whom he had accompanied on the Crusades, and then Chancellor to King John, and is considered to be one of the great statesmen of the Middle Ages.

It is also thought that Hubert Walter and Herbert Poore might jointly have conceived the idea of moving the cathedral to its present site, and that a plan for a new cathedral and town could have already been in existence by the end of the twelfth century.

MID THIRTEENTH-CENTURY TILES *depicting Richard I and Saladin fighting during the Crusades. (British Museum)*

# LAST DAYS AT OLD SARUM

**D**URING the second half of the twelfth century the clergy were becoming more disenchanted with their situation at Old Sarum. 'Without rain, dew, flowers or grass, where no nightingale sings, where there is only the castle and the wind', lamented one of the canons.

Following the disgrace and death of Bishop Roger and the clergy's loss of

OLD SARUM, *seen as outmoded. Reconstruction drawing by P. Dunn. (English Heritage)*

HERBERT POORE.
*(Salisbury Cathedral
Works Department)*

RICHARD POORE.
*(Salisbury Cathedral
Works Department)*

CANTERBURY CATHEDRAL: *the new Gothic architecture.*
*(A. F. Kersting)*

control over the castle, the relationship with its garrison progressively deteriorated. Successive kings visited rarely and the soldiers, mainly mercenaries, were bored and ill-disciplined. Continual taunting of the clergy provided good sport. Towards the end of the century, Herbert

WINCHESTER CATHEDRAL
*The west front. (A. F. Kersting)*

Poore, by then the bishop, took advantage of one of Richard the Lionheart's rare visits to England to petition for a new site. Archbishop Hubert Walter, Herbert's predecessor at Old Sarum, welcomed the plan and permission was easily obtained. Sadly, Richard died shortly afterwards and the troubled reign of his successor, King John, was not considered by the cautious Herbert to be an appropriate time for such a radical move, particularly as the king was unlikely to agree the substantial finance rechoird for such an ambitious project. Nothing happened until Herbert was succeeded by his rather more energetic brother, Richard Poore, and the Pope had been petitioned by the canons of Old Sarum in 1217.

There was a passionate litany of grievances about Old Sarum, 'continually shaken by the collision of the winds'. Prayers and singing could not be heard above the noise, and the roof of the old cathedral had to be constantly repaired. There was an acute shortage of water and the dazzling light on bare chalk caused blindness. A cynic might ask why it had taken the clergy at Old Sarum so

many years to discover these hardships, particularly since similar conditions prevailed at Durham and Lincoln.

The true reasons prompting the desire for a move were probably very different. There simply was not the space available to expand at Old Sarum, yet practical necessity must appear politically correct and material gain given an appropriate righteous gloss; medieval clergy were past masters at public relations. A new architectural movement creating far larger churches was evident across England from Canterbury to Lincoln, but most particularly in the neighbouring dioceses of Wells and Winchester. The latter had a nave 200 feet longer than that of Old Sarum. A great new cathedral needed space not just for its own ecclesiastical buildings but also for the surrounding town rechoird to support the cathedral including rents derived from property and the revenue from operating markets.

The proposed new site was described by Henry of Avranches as 'one that Adam would have preferred to paradise'; medieval clergy were equally skilled at hype.

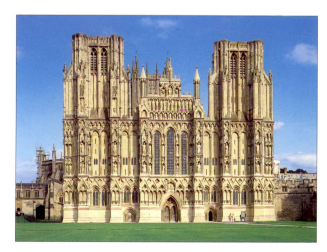

WELLS CATHEDRAL: *The west front. (A. F. Kersting)*

KING JOHN'S SEAL.
*(Salisbury Cathedral
Works Department)*

# A CHANGING WORLD

THE first 30 years of the thirteenth century witnessed a prolonged period of turmoil accompanied by profound political and social change right across England, with Salisbury very much at centre stage. During this time an intricate, three-cornered power struggle was being waged between the monarchy, the aristocracy, and the church. The relentless conflict between King John and his nobles led first to civil war and then to the historic meeting at Runnymede and the signing of the Magna Carta in 1215, an event witnessed by both William Longespee, Earl of Salisbury, and Elias of Dereham, canon and possible mastermind of the new cathedral. Today, one of only four surviving original copies of the Magna Carta is displayed in Salisbury Cathedral's Chapter House.

The trial of strength between the church and the crown had previously resulted in the brutal murder of Archbishop Thomas à Becket at Canterbury Cathedral, an atrocity which had profoundly shocked the entire Christian world. Elias of Dereham shared in the construction of the shrine which eventually contained Becket's remains. In 1220 he and Bishop Roger Poore attended the solemn ceremony in which the body was transferred from the crypt to the shrine.

King John was also being pressurised by the Pope who wished to exercise greater authority over England's affairs; the mutterings of the nobles, 'not wishing to be subject to the laws of Rome', has a familiar Eurosceptic ring. The hapless king lost his crown while crossing the Wash and also a large part of the overseas domain established by his father, Henry II, stretching from Scotland to the Pyrenees. William Longespee was one of the king's defeated generals and this embarrassing loss of French territory led to a period of anti-European sentiment in England. Meanwhile, the effect of England languishing under a Papal interdict during John's reign effectively postponed the commencement of the new Salisbury Cathedral by almost a decade.

By the early thirteenth century leadership was already shifting from the monasteries to secular cathedrals like Salisbury, while scholarship was moving from the abbeys and monasteries to the embryonic seats of learning in the newly founded universities at Oxford and Cambridge. Later that century, a group of scholars fleeing riots in Oxford came to Salisbury and founded the College of Valley Scholars; but the glorious prospect of a third university receded when the scholars returned to Oxford.

The development of the churches of the western world was being influenced by a major new architectural movement that was later to be termed Gothic. The conception of the new cathedral at Salisbury happily coincided with the time that this highly significant period of architecture was approaching a pinnacle of creative endeavour.

THE MAGNA CARTA.
*(A. F. Kersting)*

CANTERBURY CATHEDRAL
*The west towers from the south east. (A. F. Kersting)*

THIRTEENTH-CENTURY DEPICTION *of the murder of Thomas à Becket. (British Library. Harley Ee50f30)*

# ON THE MOVE

THE idea of moving the cathedral to a place more conducive to the rechoirments of thirteenth-century England was considerably eased by the fact that Bishop Richard Poore owned land that formed an eminently suitable location on a bend of the River Avon close to where it joins the River Nadder, a few miles to the south of Old Sarum. The whole site was conveniently level and sufficiently spacious to accommodate the proposed cathedral, Bishop's Palace, and the houses for the canons, together with a completely new purpose-built town; a castle was not deemed to be necessary. Underneath the topsoil, many feet of impacted river gravel provided a perfect foundation for such an enterprise.

The period of the move from Old Sarum was documented in great detail by William de Wanda, the Dean at the time. The present site had always been the preferred location in Richard Poore's scheme. While there were stories of the Bishop failing to persuade the Abbess of Wilton to provide a site – 'Hath not the Bishop land of his own that he might needs spoil the Abbess?' – such tales are less fanciful than the Bishop's vision of the Virgin Mary commanding him to build his new church at a place called Mayfield, or the site being chosen at random by firing an arrow from the ramparts of Old Sarum.

While reality is invariably more mundane than such fantasies, the new cathedral does provide a marvellous example of ambition and opportunity happily coinciding. There beckoned a perfect place, both practical and exceedingly beautiful, and Bishop Richard Poore was on hand to transfer dream into reality, assembling a handpicked group of eminent canons to assist him in his great enterprise. The new king, young Henry III, was the most generous of monarchs when endowing new cathedrals, an example quickly followed by many of the nation's great and good. Stephen Langton, the Archbishop of Canterbury, was a long-time mentor of Bishop Poore. Thus both Crown and Church favoured this ambitious project. Above all, construction was begun at a time when improving technology was greatly assisting the creative development of a superb new style of architecture.

Fate had conspired to provide highly favourable circumstances to support this venture and an opportunity existed to create something truly memorable. 'A piece of architecture of such singular and translucent beauty as not to be equalled by any structure of its bulk and age.' Posterity was not to be disappointed.

On All Saints Day 1219 work commenced on the mighty task of constructing the new cathedral on the water meadows down in the valley by the river, within sight of Old Sarum.

RIGHT: WILLIAM NAISH'S 1716 MAP *of Salisbury; note the grid plan. (Salisbury Museum)*

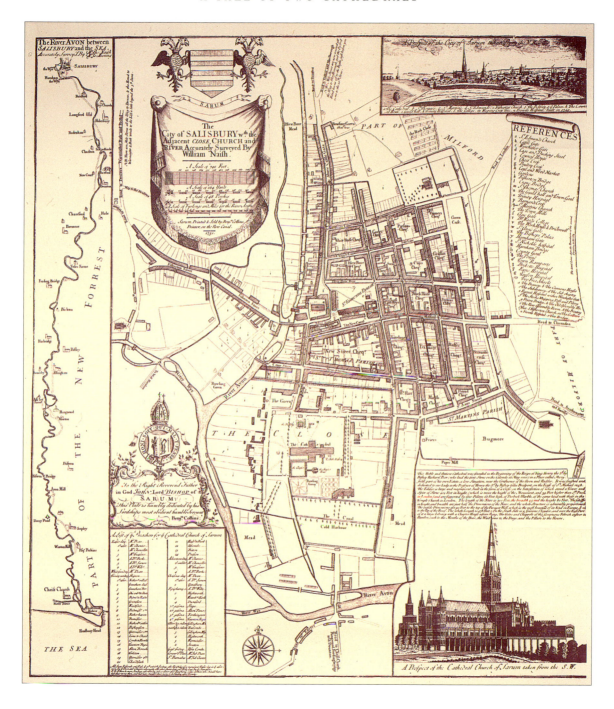

POORE FAMILY *Coat of Arms.*
*(Salisbury Cathedral Works*
*Department)*

# PORTRAIT OF A MEDIEVAL BISHOP

RICHARD POORE was the archetypal bishop of the Middle Ages – scholarly, shrewd, a born organiser, a skilful judge of character, a man of vision with a sense of mission. As Dean and Bishop of Old Sarum and the first bishop of the new cathedral, he exercised an enormous and lasting influence on the creation of the ultimate Gothic achievement that lies on the banks of the River Avon today. 'A man of outstanding

RECENT WINDOW *in choir aisle depicting Bishop Poore laying the*
*foundation stone. (Salisbury Cathedral Works Department)*

holiness and profound knowledge', the renowned chronicler Matthew Paris was later to declare. Like his brother Herbert, whom he succeeded as Bishop at Old Sarum, Richard had been born an illegitimate son of Richard of Ilchester, later the Bishop of Winchester, the wealthiest see in the country. Richard studied at Paris

University under Stephen Langton, who was later to become Archbishop of Canterbury. Having gained his mastership, he went directly to Old Sarum as Dean, finding the cathedral in a poor state with both morale and discipline in considerable disarray. He set about correcting

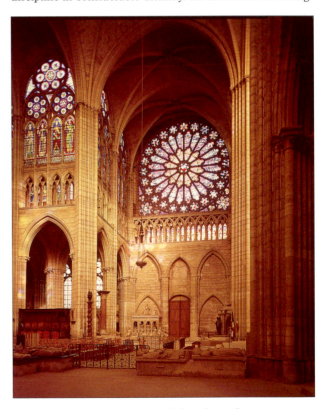

CATHEDRAL OF ST. DENIS, PARIS *from the north transept.*
*(A. F. Kersting)*

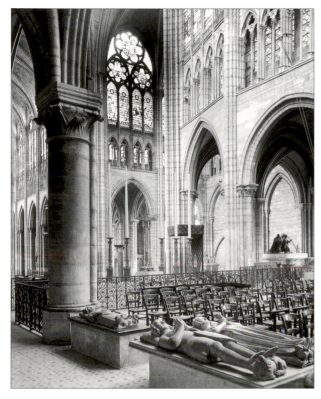

CATHEDRAL OF ST. DENIS, PARIS. *Looking into the choir, from the south aisle. (A. F. Kersting)*

this with such vigour that, before he left to become Bishop of Chichester, the cathedral at Old Sarum 'shone like the sun in full orb'.

Richard Poore was responsible for developing and refining Bishop Osmund's concepts for the liturgy, more latterly known as the 'Use of Sarum'. Such pioneering work characterised his growing reputation as both reformer and inspirational leader, so when Bishop Herbert died in January 1217, the Chapter immediately and unanimously elected Richard as his successor. The ideal choice had been made for the man who would develop the new cathedral.

## *Gothic* GENIUS

*When Abbot Suger rebuilt the choir at St Denis near Paris in the mid twelfth century, he created what has come to be considered the first example of Gothic architecture, a development as important as, and arguably more radical than, the Renaissance, and one which was to have a profound and lasting impact on the cultural landscape of western Europe. This all-powerful abbot, son of a Norman peasant, rose to become Regent of France, arch-rival of Bernard of Clairvaux, 'capable of governing the universe', according to an enthusiastic contemporary commentator.*

*Even without this extravagant endorsement, Suger's St Denis was indeed right at the cutting edge of the new technology. A far greater understanding of the principles of stone construction led to the elimination of heavy walls for load-bearing purposes. Instead, stone canopies or vaults were upheld by tall piers that took the strain while the stress of the quadripartite vaulting dispersed externally onto flying buttresses stabilised with heavy pinnacles.*

*The essential hallmarks of Gothic architecture were tall slender columns, pointed arches, rib vaulting, and spiky pinnacles, resulting in far greater height within interiors progressively better lit through ever larger windows of gloriously coloured glass. St Denis, slender and sublimely sophisticated, was consecrated in 1144, immediately condemning anything Romanesque to appear squat, heavy, and very gloomy.*

# DAWN OF THE NEW CATHEDRAL

THE foundation stones of the new cathedral were laid on April 28, 1220 at a solemn yet spectacular ceremony during which five stones were laid. The event was described in great detail by Dean William de Wanda: 'The bishop laid the first stone for our Lord the Pope Honorius, and the second for the Lord Stephen Langton, Archbishop of Canterbury and Cardinal of the Holy Roman Church, at that time with our Lord the King in the Marches of Wales, then added to the new fabric a third stone for himself. William Longespee, Earl of Sarum, who was then present, laid the fourth stone, and Ela, Countess of Sarum, the wife of the said earl, a woman truly pious and worthy because she was filled with the fear of the Lord, laid the fifth.'

It had been hoped that Henry III and the Archbishop would attend, but urgent court business took them elsewhere. Bishop Poore considered postponing the event but such were the crowds, 'a great multitude of the common people coming from all parts', that the bishop cleverly turned the occasion into a joyous festival for the people, walking barefoot through the enormous gathering as in a modern day royal walkabout.

By the time of Longespee's death the building of the cathedral was sufficiently advanced for three altars to be consecrated in 1225 in the newly built Trinity Chapel while Archbishop Langton preached to the congregation. About that time too, the tombs of three former bishops of

Old Sarum, Osmund, Jocelyn, and Roger, were brought down to the new cathedral where they can still be seen, retaining an important link between the old and new cathedrals.

The pace of construction was maintained in spite of Richard Poore reluctantly becoming Bishop of Durham in 1228. His successor, Richard Bingham, Canon Elias of Dereham, and master mason Nicholas of Ely all died in 1246. By 1258 the main walls and roofs were complete, enough for Archbishop Boniface to consecrate the cathedral in the presence of Henry III and Queen Eleanor. Bishop Roger de Mortival's Book of Statutes notes: 'It was completed on the twenty fifth of March in the year 1266, the whole expense of the fabric having been 42,000 marks'. No other completely new cathedral was to be built in England until St Paul's in the late seventeenth century.

HENRY III *as depicted in stained glass in Canterbury Cathedral. (Sonia Halliday)*

ABOVE: WILLIAM LONGESPEE.
*(Salisbury Cathedral Works Department)*

## A Christian SOLDIER

*William Longespee, Earl of Salisbury, was half brother to King John and uncle to the new young Henry III, born as a result of Henry II's love affair with Rosamund the Fair. The earl was a deeply religious warrior who had been on the Crusades to the Holy Land and had fought valiantly for King John in France. Both he and his wife, Ela, were devout Christians and dedicated patrons of the new cathedral, and convinced many other local worthies, such as Alice Brewer, to help finance its construction. Sadly, the earl did not have long to observe the building's progress. He died at his castle at Old Sarum just six years after the foundation ceremony, supposedly poisoned on the orders of Hugh de Burgh,* éminence grise *behind the young king's throne in the early years of his reign. Thus the earl became the first person to be buried in the new cathedral in 1226; his tomb remains there to this day. His widow, Ela, became a nun at Lacock Abbey, an Augustinian religious house which she had previously founded. Two sons became canons, one of whom, Nicholas Longespee, was later elected Bishop of Salisbury.*

WILLIAM LONGESPEE.
*(Salisbury Cathedral Works Department)*

23

# WHO BUILT SALISBURY CATHEDRAL?

**S**CHOLARS have spent a great deal of time
debating precisely who was the guiding force
behind the creation of the new Salisbury
Cathedral. There were no architects as such in medieval
Europe; indeed the profession did not formally exist in
England until Robert Adam and some colleagues formed
the Architect's Club in 1791, which was to become the
Royal Institute of British Architects. Even in the late
seventeenth century, the era of Wren, Vanbrugh, and
Hawksmoor, it was the master mason who translated ideas
into reality. In the Middle Ages craftsmen were held in far
greater esteem than today, and the master mason was
undoubtedly the key protagonist involved in any major
building. In the case of Salisbury Cathedral very little is
known about the master mason apart from his name,
Nicholas of Ely.

The scholastic spotlight turns therefore towards Elias
of Dereham, a very well connected canon, who lived in
Salisbury for 25 years after the foundation of the new
cathedral, having conceivably first gone to Old Sarum in
1189 when Hubert Walter became bishop there. Elias had
been born in Dereham, Norfolk, the same place as Walter,
to whom he became steward. Walter later became
Archbishop of Canterbury and Elias was present when
Walter was rebuilding the choir. After Walter's death he
served under Archbishop Stephen Langton and is thought to
have been taught by him, alongside Richard Poore in Paris.

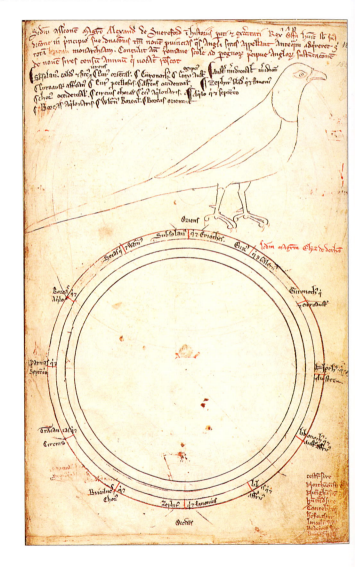

Elias' claim to fame as an architect stems from the historian Matthew Paris's description of him as, 'incomparabilis artifex'; yet this was in connection with the construction of Thomas à Becket's shrine at Canterbury rather than a great building. The king is also said to have employed Elias to work at Clarendon Palace in Wiltshire and the Great Hall at Winchester. In precisely what capacity? Designer? Clerk of Works? Surveyor? Project Manager? Elias was certainly well travelled, an enlightened intellectual who had witnessed much of the new cathedral building at Canterbury, Lincoln, and Wells; but did that qualify him as an architect in any sense of the word?

Many years later, during the Renaissance, it was customary to call on highly creative men to add artistic flair to the mason's craft. Michelangelo as a sculptor had an intimate knowledge of stone. Leonardo, in addition to being an artist, was also a brilliant scientist and engineer. Wren may have been Professor of Astronomy at Oxford but he was also a mathematician who could draw exquisitely. Elias on the other hand was educated in theology and the law.

The eminent architectural historian, Sir Nikolaus Pevsner, felt that Elias should be considered seriously as the cathedral's most likely designer, and more recently Professor Adrian Hasting has eloquently argued the case for Elias as the architect of Salisbury Cathedral.

The Bishop's influence on the development of the cathedral must not, however, be underestimated.

Richard Poore, a sophisticated, perceptive man, acutely aware of the architectural revolution taking place in western Europe at the time, would have had a constant close involvement in the shaping of the cathedral. Poore had been to Rome as well as Paris. He would probably have seen St Denis and other new cathedrals in the Ile de France and would have noted the classical remains in Italy. Might this account for the relative simplicity of Salisbury's design?

Whether Nicholas of Ely, Elias of Dereham, or even Richard Poore was the true designer of the cathedral remains a matter of continuing conjecture. An indisputable fact, however, is that its conception was a glorious work of genius.

THE CATHEDRAL *and the former Bishop's Palace, now the Cathedral School.*
*(Peter Brimacombe)*

LEFT: THE WINDROSE OF ELIAS,
*as copied by Matthew Paris. The attribution to*
*'master Elyas de Derham' is just above the rose to the right.*
*(British Library. Cotton Nero D1f185r)*

# CROWNING GLORY

I T is perhaps surprising that at the time Bishop Mortival considered the main building of the cathedral to be complete, its most famous feature did not exist. Instead of a dramatic spire soaring more than 400 feet towards the heavens there was a short stumpy lantern tower, barely visible above the roof line.

For many years it was thought that there was a considerable gap between 1266 and the construction of the present tower and octagonal spire; indeed, even Pevsner thought that this did not take place until well into the next century. Perceived wisdom today considers this to be incorrect, with the building of the taller tower and spire probably having started in the last few years of the thirteenth century.

Certainly by that time spires had become an architectural status symbol and all over England, from Old St Paul's in London to Lincoln Minster, these unique

SALISBURY CATHEDRAL.
*Looking up inside the spire, showing the wooden frame supports.*
*(A. F. Kersting)*

English contributions to the language of architecture were climbing towards heaven like so many medieval skyscrapers. They were usually constructed in wood covered in lead, whereas Salisbury's spire was stone-faced, a factor which would stand it in good stead as other more ambitious spires literally over-reached themselves and came crashing down. A stone-faced tower and spire with the masonic blocks held by iron clamps set in lead stood a better chance of survival when struck by lightning, a greater danger in the days before lightning conductors. Lightning was to strike several times at Salisbury, most seriously in 1559 when it tore out a huge gash 60 feet long, and again on 21 June, 1742, when the verger discovered a fire described by Francis Price, the Clerk of Works, as 'roaring like that when the baker is preparing his oven for bread'. Fortunately the fire was successfully dowsed.

To build a tall tower and spire in the Middle Ages was to explore the upper limits of medieval technology. Lincoln's spire, topping 525 feet, was the tallest building in the known world, outstripping the Great Pyramid by a considerable margin. Little was known of aerodynamics, though Elias of Dereham had written a poem about winds. There was only timber scaffolding and no mechanised machinery – nearly everything was done from the inside by hand.

These were the conditions that existed in medieval Salisbury, yet early in the fourteenth century the spire was complete. Nearly 700 years later, this architectural icon of western Europe remains an eloquent testimony to the vision, the faith, and the expertise of superb craftsmen. Today the medieval internal wood scaffolding is still to be seen within a spire described by a contemporary historian as, 'the greatest and most exhilarating high medieval Gothic structure, one of the architectural and engineering masterpieces of the Middle Ages'.

ABOVE: ROY SPRING *scaling the tower*
(*Salisbury Cathedral Works Department*)

LEFT: A MEMBER *of the Cathedral Works Department checking the spire.* (*Salisbury Cathedral Works Department*)

# THE ARCHITECTURE OF SALISBURY CATHEDRAL

**S**ALISBURY Cathedral represents the fulfilment of a unique architectural opportunity that occurred in the relatively short period of time between the end of the troubled reign of King John and the devastating onset of the Black Death which wiped out more than a third of the population – numerous skilled craftsmen among them.

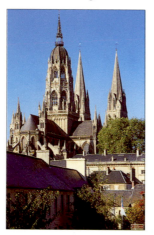 

THREE FRENCH GOTHIC CATHEDRALS: (*above left*) *Abbey of Bayeux;* (*above right*) *the east end of Notre-Dame;* (*far right*) *Rouen.* (*all Peter Brimacombe*)

Virtually all the nation's great Gothic ecclesiastical masterpieces occupy the same sites as the original Norman cathedrals. Many were only partial reconstructions or the product of long-running building programmes spanning several architectural periods. Salisbury was on a completely new site containing no other buildings and totally free from the constraints of existing fabric or foundations. Huge sums of money were raised. The construction period was relatively short, virtually continuous, and fulfilled in one architectural period to a single design that suffered no significant modifications or additions subsequent to its completion in the early fourteenth century.

Salisbury Cathedral thus conveys unity of style, symmetry of layout, and above all simple uniform completeness. Nikolaus Pevsner wrote, 'the purest Early English work is to be found at Salisbury', going on to say, 'the architecture of England between 1250 and 1350 was, although the English do not know it, the most forward, the most important and inspired in Europe'.

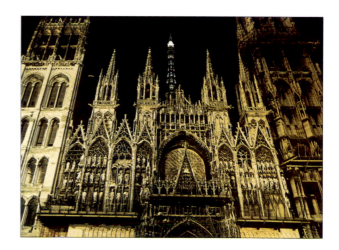

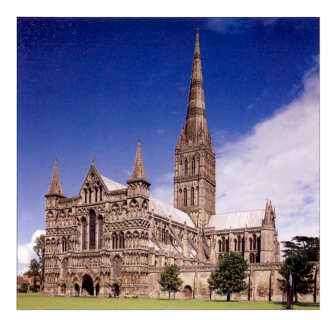

SALISBURY CATHEDRAL *from the south west. (A. F. Kersting)*

Herbert Poore's failure to instigate the move to a new site when the idea was first envisaged was advantageous in ensuring Salisbury's architectural pre-eminence. His delay meant that the implications of the initial Gothic building in England at Wells, Lincoln, and Canterbury could be fully absorbed and combined with an appreciation of the subsequent development of the High Gothic period in France where definitive cathedrals such as Notre-Dame in Paris, Rheims, and Chartres were under construction. The latter was completed as work at Salisbury began. Salisbury's design embraced the essence of French High Gothic, yet refined it in such a way that it conveyed an image that was completely English, much as Constable was influenced by continental art yet produced paintings that totally reflected English culture.

Fundamental to the architecture of a cathedral is its overall purpose. A theatre is built to perform plays, while a cathedral exists primarily as a place of formal worship on a grand scale. Thus the liturgy drove everything, and functional usage always took precedence over purely aesthetic considerations. Salisbury Cathedral was conceived to stage the 'Use of Sarum' so its creators designed from inside to out, just as Richard Rogers and other contemporary architects do today. In Salisbury's case this was carried out with particular care; the skilful use of space and the resulting balanced geometry of the interior are key factors which make the cathedral so unique. Salisbury has pure clean lines, projecting a classic simplicity that deliberately ignores the exuberance of Lincoln. Confident, relaxed, timeless, it is a cathedral built in a reflective period of English history to represent not mere vain triumphalism but an assured reaffirmation of a particular expression of faith first established at Old Sarum.

WELLS CATHEDRAL *the west front. (A. F. Kersting)*

# DECLINE AND FALL OF OLD SARUM

HARNHAM MILL.
*(Peter Brimacombe)*

THE new town of Salisbury grew rapidly around the cathedral, brimming with prestige and prosperity. The prestige derived from association with the cathedral, the Bishop's Palace, and the royal residence at nearby Clarendon. Prosperity came from the developing wool industry: firstly the export of fleeces to the continent, then the production of cloth for which the mills rechoird a constant supply of running water as a source of power. Situated among a network of five rivers, Salisbury was well placed for this new business and Harnham Mill is a relic from those days.

Inadequate water supply was one of the factors that had driven the clerics out of Old Sarum. Now its citizens drifted away to pastures new and better living conditions down in the valley, attracted by a new form of employment that Old Sarum could not provide. The old cathedral and Bishop's Palace lay forlorn and abandoned, the castle became a prison, a once vibrant town declined and decayed. In the mid fourteenth century the old cathedral was demolished and the stone used to construct the walls and gateways around the Cathedral Close in new Salisbury. By the end of the fifteenth century Salisbury was the fourth largest city in southern England behind London, Bristol, and Exeter, while Old Sarum lay almost deserted. When Henry VIII's emissary John Leland visited some years later, he could not find one house within Old Sarum that was inhabited, and the castle lay in ruins. Samuel Pepys, visiting Salisbury on 10 June, 1668, noted in his diary, 'so over the plain by the site of the steeple, to Salisbury by night, but before I came to the town I saw a great fortification and there light, and to it, and in it, and find it prodigious, so as to fright me to be in it alone at that time of night, it being dark, I understand since to be called Old Sarum'.

THE PLAQUE *commemorating the spot where Members of Parliament for Old Sarum were elected. (English Heritage)*

Old Sarum was to live on in a somewhat bizarre manner as one of the most notorious 'rotten boroughs' in the whole of England, continuing to be represented at Westminster by two Members of Parliament well into the nineteenth century, despite being devoid of population.

By then Old Sarum had become privately owned so the landlord could manipulate the election, certain that a candidate, invariably himself, would duly become one of the Members of Parliament for Old Sarum. The landlord granted short leases on two plots of land and the tenants, now *bona fide* voters, cast their votes in a tent erected under a huge elm, known as the Parliament Tree, standing in the old market place. Duty done, they duly resigned their tenancies for a small consideration.

William Pitt the Elder, later Earl of Chatham and the nation's leader in the mid eighteenth century, represented Old Sarum between 1734 and 1747. William Pitt the Younger, one of England's most famous politicians, later campaigned unsuccessfully to abolish the rotten boroughs,

failing for the third time with a bill introduced in 1785. Nearly 50 years later Lord Russell succeeded after three attempts in the face of determined opposition from the Tories, the House of Lords, and most particularly the Duke of Wellington. Twenty-one bishops also voted against the motion. Lord Russell pointed out that Old Sarum, returning two members to the House of Commons, 'was only a green mound without habitation on it', whereas major cities like Birmingham and Manchester had no parliamentary representation whatsoever. He was supported by Lord Macaulay's passionate speech which contained the succinct words, 'the public's enthusiasm is undiminished. Old Sarum has grown no bigger, Manchester has grown no smaller!' The Reform Act finally became law on June 7, 1832. Old Sarum's demise was complete.

CARICATURE *showing those for and against the 1832 Reform Bill. 'Old Sarum' appeared on one of the lower left-hand branches. (British Museum)*

HENRY HYDE COAT OF ARMS *circa 1650.*
*(Salisbury Cathedral Works Department)*

# CATHEDRAL IN PERIL

**W**HILE Old Sarum was in terminal decline the new city of Salisbury grew and prospered. Yet the new town's success and that of the cathedral were to be threatened by a series of

STATUE OF OLIVER
CROMWELL.
*(Peter Brimacombe)*

traumatic events during the sixteenth and seventeenth centuries, most particularly the Reformation and the bitter Civil War between the king and Parliament which led to the nation becoming a republic for the only time in its history.

As a secular cathedral, Salisbury came through the Reformation relatively unscathed compared with monastic foundations such as Winchester, Durham, and Canterbury. These all had to revise their constitutions. Salisbury's was kept intact, and it thus came to be known as a Cathedral of the Old Foundation, like York and Chichester, which were also secular establishments.

After the break with Rome, Henry VIII dismissed Cardinal Campeggio as Bishop of Salisbury while one of the canons, unwise enough to preach against the

Reformation, was hung drawn and quartered. This fate also befell the elderly abbot at nearby Glastonbury Abbey, after first being dragged up Glastonbury Tor bound to a sheep hurdle. The wily Vicar of Bray was a resident canon at Salisbury during these dangerous time when the sacred shrine of St Osmund was destroyed, as was that of Thomas à Becket which Elias of Dereham had created at Canterbury Cathedral. The 'Use of Sarum', which Osmund had initiated, was replaced by the English Prayer Book together with a completely new form of service.

The Civil War had more serious consequences for the cathedral. Fighting took place in the Close, Parliamentarian troops plundered the cathedral in 1644, and further damage to the cloisters and Chapter House was inflicted by Dutch prisoners. Normal cathedral life

WEST FRONT, HEALE HOUSE. *(Peter Brimacombe)*

EXTRACT *from Sir Christopher Wren's Notebook.*
*(Salisbury Cathedral Library)*

came to a virtual halt as canons left to join the Royalist forces and there was to be little improvement during Cromwell's reign as Protector. It was during this period that Christopher Wren's father, a vicar in the diocese at nearby East Knoyle, was tried for heresy. When found guilty he was heavily fined and removed from office.

## A renewed CUSTOM

*One of the ancient ceremonies that King Henry VIII had abolished during the Reformation was the custom of electing a 'Boy Bishop'. Every December for three weeks, a boy chorister was elected by his fellow choristers to sit on the bishop's throne, preach a sermon, and conduct a service. The names of 24 Boy Bishops were recorded in the register. Thankfully this intriguing custom has recently been partially revived and once again, for one glorious day in December, the head choirboy presides over the cathedral as Boy Bishop.*

When Charles II was restored as king, the Cathedral, the Bishop's Palace, and the houses of the canons were in a sorry state of repair, despite heroic efforts by the Hyde family of nearby Heale House, who had secretly funded repairs to the cathedral. By this time the morale in the city was at its lowest ebb since the foundation. However, cometh the hour, cometh the man – in this instance a highly charismatic new bishop, Doctor Seth Ward.

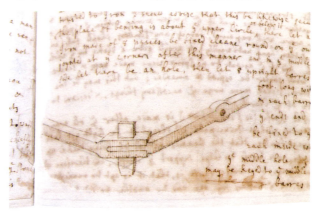

EXTRACT *from Sir Christopher Wren's Notebook.*
*(Salisbury Cathedral Library)*

# PORTRAIT OF A SEVENTEENTH-CENTURY BISHOP

**D**OCTOR Seth Ward had been Sir Christopher Wren's predecessor as Professor of Astronomy at Oxford University, having originally taken his degree at Sidney Sussex, Cambridge. Ward and Wren had first met while at All Souls, Oxford. Both were outstanding scholars. Ward was a brilliant mathematician and philosopher, founder member of the Royal Society, and author of a definitive work on the orbital nature of planets. In addition to Wren, his circle of friends included Isaac Newton, Thomas Hobbes, Samuel Pepys, and King Charles II. The king once visited Salisbury and, having watched a football match, climbed to the top of the cathedral tower and saw a sailor ascend

BISHOP *Seth Ward circa 1667. (R. Parker)*

the spire and stand on his head on the capstone. Charles refused the sailor any money on the grounds that this would encourage further daredevil antics!

Ward was appointed Bishop of Salisbury at the age of 50 in 1667, having previously been Bishop of Exeter. Almost single-handedly, he set about restoring the cathedral, contributing generously

NORTH GATE, *High Street, Salisbury. (Peter Brimacombe)*

from his own pocket. He was a charitable man and founded the almshouses known as the College of Matrons between the North Gate and the Close. Ward was 'a most magnificent and munificent mind', according to John Aubrey, the seventeenth-century antiquary, and the cathedral became known for 'excellent preaching, divine service being celebrated with exemplary decorum and celestial music'.

Bishop Ward was concerned with the structural state of the cathedral, particularly the tower and spire. 6500 tones pressing down on columns and foundations, built long before such a tall spire had been envisaged, had distorted the columns and caused the foundations to sink on one side, resulting in the spire being out of alignment by nearly two feet. Christopher Wren conducted an exhaustive structural survey and his detailed, very lucid notes can still be seen in the cathedral library. Wren prescribed remedial treatment concluding with the succinct comment, 'brace ye spire towards ye top with iron'. It was a wise precaution, even though the spire was not in imminent danger of collapse, for it has not subsided further and remains the tallest spire in England, while other originally taller spires at Malmesbury, Old St Paul's, and Lincoln are no longer standing.

The bishop was highly eccentric and an acute hypochondriac, given to wild 20-mile gallops on horseback across the Downs. His recipe for curing gout was 'take an old fat cat, flea it, draw forth the guts, then beat it well with a rolling pin and anoint to afflicted parts'.

Bishop Ward's worst failing, however, was his nepotism. He appointed numerous members of his family to clerical positions in the diocese, an unfortunate series of events which eventually led to a long and bitter quarrel with Dean Pierce, and marred the reputation of the man who did so much to revive the fortunes of the cathedral and the city in the wake of Cromwell and the Civil War.

## The College of MATRONS

*Within the Cathedral Close, just inside the fourteenth-century High Street Gate, are the almshouses built in the late seventeenth century for the widows of the clergy of the dioceses of Exeter and Salisbury, a function that they still fulfil today. It has been said that Sir Christopher Wren designed the college. There is no proof of this, but the jaunty cupola echoes Wren's other cupolas atop the chapel of Emmanuel College, Cambridge, and the Sheldonian at Oxford. It is rather less likely that Wren Hall can be attributed to him. This fine Queen Anne building once housed the Choristers' School and gave its name to the green adjacent to Mompesson House.*

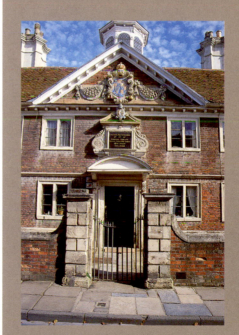

COLLEGE OF MATRONS.
*(Peter Brimacombe)*

# THE CLOSE IN SALISBURY

THE beauty of the cathedral is much enhanced by its setting, a tranquil oasis of immaculately cut turf and slender lines of chestnut trees surrounded by houses that parade the best of English domestic architecture over many centuries.

This is the Close whose origins date back to the foundation of the new cathedral. When Bishop Poore moved down from Old Sarum he created a palace for himself and instructed the canons to build houses for themselves in the area immediately around the huge construction site of the new cathedral. The majority of the canons were relatively well off,

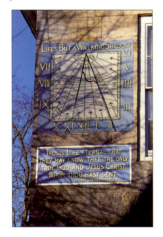

MALMESBURY HOUSE
SUNDIAL.
*(Peter Brimacombe)*

deriving considerable income from their estates, and their houses reflected both their wealth and their status.

By 1331 authority had been obtained from Edward III to enclose the area with a wall built from stone brought down from the ruins of the old cathedral at Sarum. By the end of the Middle Ages most houses belonged to the bishop or the Dean and Chapter and were allocated to the canons in order of seniority, or even let to privileged citizens of the town. Today houses such as Hemyngsby on Choristers' Green and Aula

MALMESBURY HOUSE.
*(Peter Brimacombe)*

le Stage on the North Walk of the Close still show traces of their medieval origins, as does the Old Deanery, now known as the Medieval Hall, although the medieval remains of Leadenhall, originally Elias of Dereham's house on the West Walk, have disappeared under Victorian stucco. Next door is the South Canonry, home of the present bishop, the original palace having become the Cathedral School shortly after the Second World War. There are a number of other educational establishments in the Close including Sarum College on the North Walk and the nearby Bishop Wordworth's School.

Many other properties in the Close fell into disrepair during the Civil War and the extensive rebuilding that took place at the time of the Restoration reflects this exquisite

THE WALTON CANONRY.
*(Peter Brimacombe)*

period of English architecture. Mompesson House, now owned by the National Trust, was completed in 1701; the Walton Canonry was the house where Isaac Walton, author of *The Compleat Angler*, lived with his son, a canon at the cathedral in the mid eighteenth century. Malmesbury House, adjacent to St Anne's Gate, was built at a similar time and became the property of James 'Hermes' Harris, so nicknamed because he wrote a celebrated study of ancient philosophy. Harris was a highly sophisticated and cultured man, friend of Fielding and Richardson, the Restoration playwrights, David Garrick, Doctor Johnson,

MOMPESSON HOUSE.
*(Peter Brimacombe)*

ARUNDELLS.
*(Peter Brimacombe)*

and ardent admirer of Handel, whose first English concert is said to have been given in the room above St Anne's Gate. There is an eye-catching sundial on the wall of Malmesbury House depicting the Julian calendar, and the interior of the house is a riot of Rococo decoration, the bow window in the library being particularly notable.

Hungerford Chantry next door to Mompesson House was built in the mid eighteenth century, as were

MYLES PLACE.
*(Peter Brimacombe)*

Braybrooke, Arundells, and Myles Place, once the home of the distinguished historian, Sir Arthur Bryant.

The lovely expanse of turf which forms the centre of the Close is surprisingly the work of James Wyatt. 'Wrecker' Wyatt has been rightly criticised for his insensitive alterations inside the cathedral in the late eighteenth century and the removal of the bell tower on the western side of the Close. However, before he transformed the area, it was a low-lying, waterlogged graveyard. Wyatt removed the gravestones, installed drainage, and raised the level of the whole area, creating the largest and most beautiful Close in the whole of Britain, a perfect setting for the cathedral.

SALISBURY CATHEDRAL *and Close showing the detached bell tower before its demolition in the eighteenth century. (Salisbury Museum)*

# THE ART OF SALISBURY CATHEDRAL

**M**EMORABLE buildings, like beautiful landscapes, invariably inspire great art. Rouen Cathedral caught Monet's imagination, and Salisbury was a major inspiration to that outstanding pair of English landscape artists, Constable and Turner.

John Constable was a friend of Archdeacon John Fisher, then living at Leadenhall, the house originally built by Elias of Dereham. Fisher was an enthusiastic follower of contemporary art, and contemptuous of the collection of pictures belonging to the previous owner of Leadenhall, which included works by Raphael, Canaletto, Poussin, and Rembrandt. In 1819 he commissioned Constable to paint 'The White Horse' which Fisher proudly hung over the fireplace of his drawing room.

While Constable stayed with the archdeacon at Leadenhall he produced the series of sketches on which his masterly paintings of the cathedral were based. His invariable

viewpoint was across the water meadows, scenes that are still readily identifiable today. A Constable landscape painted in 1820, now hanging in the National Gallery in London, depicts the cathedral from across the river with Leadenhall clearly showing in the foreground. These

OLD SARUM *as painted by John Constable in 1834. (Victoria & Albert Museum)*

works represent the finest tradition of English landscape painting and can be seen both at the National Gallery and the Victoria and Albert Museum in London; the latter also has a particularly fine sketch of Old Sarum executed in 1834.

ROTATING GLASS PRISM
*engraved by Laurence Whistler*
*in memory of his brother, Rex.*
*(Salisbury Cathedral*
*Works Department)*

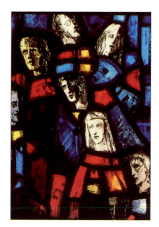

PRISONERS OF CONSCIENCE
*window. (Salisbury Cathedral*
*Works Department)*

THE CRUCIFIXION *by*
*Barbara Hepworth. (Salisbury*
*Cathedral Works Department)*

WALKING MADONNA
*by Elizabeth Frink. (Salisbury*
*Cathedral Works Department)*

Laurence Whistler's exquisite engraved glass prism, a memorial to his brother, Rex, killed in Normandy during the Second World War.

Too little of the cathedral's original stained glass remains. Having survived the wear and tear of many centuries, the Reformation, and the Civil War, much of the medieval glass was needlessly removed by James Wyatt in the late eighteenth century. However, Dean Sydney Evans had the inspired idea of engaging the great French glazier, Gabriel Loire of Chartres, to conceive the extraordinarily fine glass that now fills the East Window in the Trinity Chapel. Unveiled in May 1980 by Yehudi Menuhin, *The Prisoners of Conscience* window magically recreates the colour and richness of medieval glass in a marvellously updated contemporary manner.

Joseph Mallord William Turner was painting at the same time as Constable, having been born a year earlier in 1775. In his formative years he was greatly encouraged by the highly successful portrait painter Thomas Lawrence, whose father was landlord at the Bear, a coaching inn at nearby Devizes. Turner's painting of Salisbury Cathedral from Old Sarum, together with his delicate portrayals of the cathedral's interior, are in the Salisbury and South Wiltshire Museum which owns six of his works.

Twentieth-century art at the Cathedral is represented by Elizabeth Frink's *Walking Madonna*, sculpted in bronze and standing near the North Porch. Frink, one of the nation's outstanding modern sculptors, lived not far away in Dorset and was a friend of the late Dean Sydney Evans. Frink's own tragic early death was commemorated by a memorial service in the cathedral. Barbara Hepworth's controversial sculpture of the crucifixion was exhibited in the Close for a number of years, while inside Salisbury Cathedral is

CATHEDRAL WORKMEN
*circa 1870.*
*(Salisbury Cathedral Works
Department)*

# OUTSIDE STORY

**A**N intimate view of the exterior of the cathedral from Roy Spring, for more than 25 years the Cathedral's Clerk of Works:

Go through St Anne's Gate along the North Walk to the Close and discover what I regard as the greatest Cistercian abbey church ever created,

ST. ANNE'S GATE.
*(Peter Brimacombe)*

a simplicity of design that is quite outstanding. The view from the north-east corner of the Close shows the cathedral in the sequence in which it was built. You can see the east end where the foundation stones were laid, the gradual progression westwards, and the natural progression upwards to the spire. When the main building was finished in 1258 it was without the spire and until that was built the cathedral was not truly complete. You must remember that the original purpose was to get the building operational as a house of prayer. The spire was only a marker for people coming from a distance, while the ground floor of the cathedral was an essential part of the liturgy.

You get a continual upwards thrust; the pinnacles are over-large and over-long compared with some cathedrals, and the tower and spire complete this upward surge towards the heavens in a way that I feel is quite splendid. In 1258 there would have been the detached bell tower standing in the Close, some distance away from the north porch, a substantial building in its own right, rising some 200 feet, to within 20 feet of the height of the present tower. It certainly had ten bells and may even have had the first ring of twelve bells in the country.

The tower was removed by Wyatt in the late eighteenth century and in dry weather the foundations can be clearly seen when the grass turns brown. In 1258 the lantern tower of the cathedral would have risen just above the main roofline before building began on the tower and spire in the late thirteenth century. This remains the tallest medieval stone structure in Europe. The colour of the cathedral's Chilmark stone, quarried locally, changes with the weather, reacting to different light and moisture content. In winter it turns a greenish colour, most evident when the building is floodlit at night. In summer the stone dries out to a silvery grey, while the buttresses on the north transept have been turned a delicate pinky red by lichen, once described as the living stain upon the stone.

Another of my favourite views of the cathedral is from the south-east, from the grounds of the Cathedral School. It looks quite spectacular, with the roofs rising to the tower and spire, the treasury which has now become the vestry, and the great octagonal building of the Chapter House protruding from the end of the south transept – a delightful group of buildings in contrasting textures of dressed stone and flint representing a marvellous usage of space.

The cloister is the largest ecclesiastical cloister in the country. People wonder why Salisbury has a cloister, being a secular foundation, but they were used in exactly the same context as in a monastic foundation – providing a contemplative walk in rainy weather, and in fine weather a

place for study. It was also an important part of the processional way and processions still form up here before entering the cathedral. Originally the cloister was painted and there are still traces in the North Walk, yet to really appreciate its original beauty go into the vestibule of the Chapter House.

The niches on the west front contain eight of the original statues; the rest are all of nineteenth-century date, paid for by the local citizens. You could sponsor a statue – £45 for a small angel, £85 for an archangel! During the Civil War the statues were used for musket practice by Parliamentarian troops and the west wall of the cloister is also pockmarked with musket balls.

There is great beauty in the simplicity of the cathedral and, while a mixture of styles might appeal to some people, it is the overall symmetry of a building constructed in one piece that so appeals to me. If you are looking for the perfect building in a perfect setting, this is it.

LEFT: SOUTH VIEW *of Salisbury Cathedral from the Cloisters by J. M. W. Turner. (Victoria & Albert Museum)*

RIGHT: TOP OF SPIRE *from the south-west. (Peter Brimacombe)*

# INSIDE INFORMATION

An informative view of the cathedral's interior from Cathedral Guide, Major General Roy Dixon:

Upon entering the cathedral you see its entire length, there being no choir screen, which creates a great sense of space. The nave is one of the longest in the country and 85 feet high. Cathedrals were designed on a grand scale, both to inspire people, many of them illiterate, and to suit a liturgy composed of colourful processions.

The cathedral is constructed from two types of stone, local cream Chilmark stone and darker Purbeck 'marble' from Dorset, actually compressed fossilised freshwater snails producing an easily polished stone. The ground plan is the traditional cruciform shape, with two main transepts and two sub-transepts further eastwards.

DETAIL *from Cloister.*
*(Salisbury Cathedral Works Department)*

When walking around the cathedral the first thing you will find is the oldest working clock in England, built in 1386, which was brought into the cathedral when the exterior bell tower was demolished. Nearby is the lovely alabaster tomb of Lord Cheney, Henry Tudor's

MASON WORKING ON CHILMARK STONE.
*(Salisbury Cathedral Works Department)*

Standard Bearer at the Battle of Bosworth. After Henry became king, Cheney was to become a Member of the Order of the Garter and a baron. The tomb was opened in 1973 and he turned out to be over seven feet tall; he must have been a fearsome sight on horseback!

There are two extremely fine chests in the north transept. The muniment chest has seven locks while the lovely cope chest is one of only very few examples in England. Close by, the tomb of Bishop Blyth is a marvellous example of the medieval craftsman's humour – the long row of roses which he had been carving for weeks followed by a portrayal of himself with a bored face and a pair of shears!

DETAIL *of the lierne vaulting in the Chapter House. (Salisbury Cathedral Works Department)*

Stand under the crossing and look upwards to see how much the piers have bent supporting the colossal weight of the tower and spire. A floor plaque in the North Choir Aisle commemorates the son of Thomas Lambert, 'born 16th May 1683, died February 19th of the same year'– these were the days of the Julian calendar when the year began on March 25.

The Morning Chapel, containing part of the original screen between the choir and the nave, was built around 1230. Once highly decorated, you can still see traces of paint on the angel's wings while the faces below are another example of the medieval mason's freedom of expression – portraits of fellow masons and friends. The doors of the aumbry were probably brought from Old Sarum.

The Audley Chapel in Perpendicular style contains embroidery by the Sarum embroiderers. The carved pomegranate, an emblem of Catherine of Aragon, was overlooked when Henry VIII ordered all traces of her obliterated after their divorce.

The back row of the choir stalls with intricately carved misericords was installed when the cathedral was first built. The poppy heads are sixteenth century, the angel carvings nineteenth century, while the canopies, only

completed in 1925, depict the bishops in chronological order, the fourth from the north-east end being Cardinal Campeggio, the last Roman Catholic Bishop of Salisbury.

The Trinity Chapel, east of the High Altar, would normally be termed the Lady Chapel, but as the whole cathedral is dedicated to the Virgin Mary, this chapel is dedicated to the Trinity. The lovely wooden Madonna and Child are fourteenth century. The walls of the Trinity Chapel are original, the windows more recent; the original medieval glass was removed by Wyatt. Gabriel Loire's *Prisoners of Conscience* window, unveiled in 1980, initially appears as simply a glorious mass of colour, and it takes time to appreciate its intricate imagery. The best time to see it is early in the morning when the sun is streaming into the cathedral.

The Chapter House was built slightly later than the cathedral and contains marvellously delicate lierne vaulting on a single central stem and a thirteenth-century frieze of episodes from Genesis and Exodus. The Chapter House's unique treasure is Magna Carta, one of the four surviving original copies. The building retains its original thirteenth-century roof and vaults and shows very early English use of tracery.

THE NAVE. *(Salisbury Cathedral Works Department)*

# OLD SARUM TODAY

A BRIEF tour with Brian Davison, Senior Inspector of Ancient Monuments, South Western Region, English Heritage:

To fully appreciate Old Sarum approach from the north, across the Plain from Amesbury towards Salisbury, when suddenly the bulk of the Iron Age fort comes into view like an animal gone to sleep under the ground, just as the spire of the present cathedral appears some miles ahead.

To get an historical insight into Old Sarum, walk around the outer bailey atop the old Iron Age ramparts with the present cathedral clearly visible in the valley down below. These earthworks were built and rebuilt several times from the Iron Age through to Norman times, the entire sequence providing a series of intriguingly complex archaeological layers containing the history of the site.

The surrounding countryside bears a similar appearance to the Norman period, though in those days there would have been fewer hedges and no natural woodland. Everything was cultivated, the woods as 'tree fields' producing timber, while the decline of sheep farming in recent years has led to the rough grassland depicted in Constable's paintings becoming progressively more covered in scrub.

Walk westwards along the bank to the old rear entrance which was once protected by an outer mound or barbican

OLD SARUM: *aerial view of the Cathedral, looking north-east. (English Heritage & Skyscan Balloon Photography)*

with two wooden bridges connecting it to the outside world. Climb up the path through the remains of this gateway and you will come across the cathedral site while looking up at the castle remains high above.

The ditches are now only three quarters the depth of the originals and the ramparts would have been a quarter higher. Originally these ramparts would have been topped with an earth-backed timber palisade, just like an eleventh-century version of Fort Laramie!

The gatehouse at the eastern end forms the main entrance to the castle and is best appreciated while standing on the bridge leading to the inner bailey. This gatehouse would have been built of stone after the

Norman Conquest, entrances being potential weak points in the event of attack. Beyond the gatehouse is the inner bailey or courtyard and the castle. In addition to providing protection, castles were a form of aristocratic theatre, image projection in an age before newspapers, radio, and television, impressing the visitors with a sense of power and grandeur.

The Keep or Great Tower would have been about three times the present height, some 90 feet tall, and about half the area within the inner bailey would have been built upon, the rest paved and cobbled rather than grassed as it is today. The area is far from level because the remains of extensive buildings lie beneath the surface, originally a mixture of stone-faced buildings, flint rubble constructions, and timber-framed buildings, plastered and painted to look like stone. Today you are looking merely at the flint core of the walls – the original walls of the castle and the adjacent Royal Palace, created for William the Conqueror in wood, were subsequently rebuilt in stone and faced in ashlar during the reign of Henry I.

During very dry weather in 1834 the plan of the cathedral clearly showed up in the parched grass. The original foundations were marked out after the site had been carefully measured and partially excavated early in the twentieth century, the markings in two colours to distinguish Osmund's original building from Roger's later extension.

It is extremely unusual to find an entire cathedral site that has been abandoned in this way, yet remains so clearly visible today as an evocative reminder of a once great building – smooth-faced, sumptuously decorated, 'carved as from a single block of stone'. Romanesque architecture

invariably gave that impression because you would have been unable to detect the joints between the stone.

People have been entering through the ancient ramparts at Old Sarum for more than 2000 years and today this fascinating historic site is entrusted to the care of English Heritage to ensure it remains protected and accessible for many years to come.

EXCAVATION *of the Old Sarum site at the beginning of the century.* (*Salisbury Museum*)

# MORE THAN SEVEN CENTURIES LATER

THE cathedral has survived the passage of time remarkably well, standing up to the ravages of nature and the destructiveness of man with equal resilience. While rain, wind, and extremes of temperature have inevitably taken their toll, a great deal has been rectified during the ongoing multi-million pound restoration programme. Indeed today the appearance of much of the cathedral is so pristine that a passer-by was heard to mutter that it was looking far too new!

The cathedral has also survived the insensitive attentions of Henry VIII, Cromwell, and latterly James Wyatt and Gilbert Scott attempting to 'improve' the original perfection of Early English architecture. It is fortunate that Salisbury never became a modern industrial city, so the cathedral was spared the consequences of the pollution which industry brings in its wake. A particular delight is that Salisbury Cathedral retains its setting which has little changed for so many centuries. It presents a scene which would be immediately recognisable to Wren, Pepys, or Constable if they could return to the Cathedral Close today.

The area of the city that immediately surrounds the cathedral retains the distinctive chequer pattern, the medieval gridded street plan that Bishop Richard Poore developed all those years ago.

The appearance of some buildings can be deceptive. The frontage of King's House in the Close, so named because James I stayed there on a number of occasions, looks Tudor but in reality is nineteenth century. Today it houses the splendid Salisbury and South Wiltshire Museum. Likewise the frontage of the quaintly named Wardrobe is mid nineteenth-century 'Old English', the name indicating that the building was once the bishop's storehouse. Today it

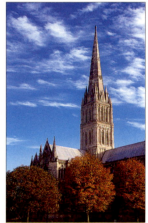

SALISBURY CATHEDRAL.
*(Peter Brimacombe)*

ORDINATION *of priests in Salisbury Cathedral.*
*(Carina Niebecker)*

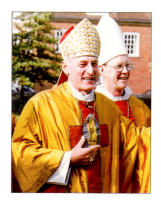

THE BISHOP *of Salisbury, the Rt. Rev. Dr. David Stancliffe, with the Bishop of Ramsbury. (Carina Niebecker)*

contains the Duke of Edinburgh's Regimental Museum.

The cathedral is still at the heart of the city and its daily life. Well over half a million visitors annually travel from all over the world, modern-day pilgrims who wonder at its grandeur and gain spiritual comfort from this centre of calm in an ever more frenetic world, with magnificent organ playing and an address from the pulpit every hour. Central to the life of the cathedral is formal worship – the great set-piece services together with special services for the diocese and for organisations ranging from Amnesty International to the Burma Star Association. The cathedral also provides the community with a venue for concerts and other cultural events and forms an important focus for the annual Salisbury Festival.

Rising high over the city and the surrounding countryside is the spire, its top appropriately the newest part, totally renewed between 1949 and 1951 with further comprehensive repairs commencing in 1987. Old Sarum can clearly be seen from the top. Roy Spring frequently climbed the spire, scaling the last feet externally via a series of iron rungs. In his own book on Salisbury Cathedral he describes the view:

'To look down from the apex of the spire gives one a sense of respect and admiration for those who built it and an indebtedness to those who have repaired it during intervening centuries. Perhaps someone else will stand there in two or three hundred years and admire the work of the late twentieth-century masons. If somebody is able to climb and stand aloft after such a period of time, we may have learnt to live correctly on this planet of ours, to have stopped our destruction of nature and perhaps the work being carried out at the present time may have helped preserve Salisbury Cathedral for further generations.'

INSIDE *Salisbury Cathedral, Songs of Praise 1987. (Salisbury Cathedral Works Department)*

# ACKNOWLEDGEMENTS

In addition to the Bishop of Salisbury, the author would like to convey grateful thanks to Canon David Durston, Tim Tatton-Brown, Brian Davison, John Chandler, Sue Eward, Major General Roy Dixon, Brian Purvis, Professor Adrian Hastings, and members of the staff at Salisbury Cathedral and Old Sarum. Particular thanks go to Roy Spring for his continuing assistance and his permission to quote from his book on the cathedral which ends this publication so appropriately.

# FURTHER READING

Tim Tatton-Brown *Great Cathedrals of Britain*

Tim Tatton-Brown *Antiquity*, volume 65

Teresa Webber *Scribes and scholars at Salisbury Cathedral, 1075 to 1125*

John Chandler *Salisbury history and guide*

John Chandler *Endless Street*

Thomas Cocke & and Peter Kidson *Salisbury Cathedral, Perspectives on architectural history*

G H Cook *Portrait of Salisbury Cathedral*

T J Northey *The popular history of Old and New Sarum*

Adrian Hastings *Elias of Dereham, architecture of Salisbury Cathedral*

H Hatcher *An historical and descriptive account of Old and New Sarum or Salisbury*

Kathleen Edwards *Salisbury Cathedral, an ecclesiastical history*

Winston Churchill *History of the English Speaking Peoples, Vol 1, The Birth of Britain*

English Heritage *Old Sarum* (guidebook)

The Pitkin Guide *Salisbury Cathedral*

Daphne Stroud *Saint Osmund of Salisbury*

Daphne Stroud *Richard Poore and the building of Salisbury Cathedral*

Roy Spring *Stained glass, Salisbury Cathedral*

Roy Spring *Salisbury Cathedral*

N Pevsner and P Metcalf *The cathedrals of England*